# My Journey Through The Solar System

Corinne Naylor

BookLeaf
Publishing

Presentation by *BookLeaf Publishing*

Web: www.bookleafpub.com

E-mail: info@bookleafpub.com

ISBN: 9789358312966

First edition 2023

# ACKNOWLEDGEMENT

Thank you to NASA who made a cool app to look at space pictures and learn about our solar system. It helped inspire my creative twist on the planets!

# I'm Leaving This Planet

My eyes open to the sound of the birds,
Their singing startling me from my sleep.
I cannot seem to remember the blur
Of dreams that swept me off my feet.

Each day is a struggle
Trying to get out of bed.
Time to work in a hustle
Which I'll do until I'm dead.

We were told all our lives
That we should break the status quo,
But when we try, hope our dies.
They don't want to lose control.

Our lives are more than the money we make,
More than our schedules and screens.
We were meant to make mistakes
And live out all of our dreams.

I'm tired of the suppression,
Of being forced in a box.
I'm sick of depression
From being who I'm not.

So I'm going to leave today,
I'm not doing this anymore.
I'm flying up up and away
And I'm going to explore!

Goodbye to the Earth,
It was nice for a while.
But it's time to feel worth
For myself every mile.

# Homemade Rocket

Today is the day
I finished building my rocket!
I'm ready to go,
A four-leaf clover in my pocket.

I strap myself in
And I start the countdown:
5, 4, 3, 2, 1,
I lift off from the ground.

My friends are all here
And they're watching me go.
I tell them, "Don't cry,
I'll be back before it snows!"

I feel so free,
Lifting up to the skies.
And I pray, "Dear Lord,
Please don't let me die."

I've made it this far
In this leap I have taken.
To turn my back now
Would leave my heart broken.

I fly higher and higher
And start to see the stars!
Getting closer and closer,
Yet they still feel so far.

One day I will get there,
I know in my heart.
Each star now shining
And glowing in the dark.

I love it, in space,
It's just what I needed.
In my rocket, it's blue,
We won't be defeated!

Through layers and layers
Of ozone and atmosphere,
I push myself forward
Until my first stop is near.

When I land safely,
I feel I'm alone.
I put on my helmet,
And gazed back to my home.

# The Moon

5

Since I was young,
I'd look up at the stars,
And shining there among them
Was the moon, so large.

She'd follow me anywhere
On walks and in cars.
I'd think of all who see her,
No matter how far.

"The moon is made of cheese,"
My friend's dad tried to tell me.
"That's not true," I would say.
My friend was so angry.

She's interesting enough
On her own fruition.
Her purpose is known
To science and superstition.

And now here I am,
Stepping onto the surface!
Weightless, I stride
And do flips like the circus.

My footprints will be here,
Forever and always,
For someone to find
In the far future days.

I take a good look
At the ground and my tracks,
And pick out my favorite
Moon rock to take back.

I wave at the Earth
To show them I'm thriving.
I picture them waving
As they watch the moon rising.

# The Sun

I got as close as I could
To the sun, mind you.
It scorched (and knew it would)
My rocket's fine blue!

My sunglasses on,
I put on my sunscreen,
And predict how long
To pop corn for a treat.


It's too hot to go further,
I'd probably burn.
But I saw it, for sure!
There's not much more to learn.

One day it'll explode
When we least expect it.
Better off not to know,
At least it's a swift exit.

# Mercury

I landed on Mercury
Just the other day.
I had to check twice,
That I went the right way.

It looks like our moon,
Only a bit hotter.
The sun here is huge,
And there is no water.

I stayed for a bit
To rest up my rocket.
So I settled myself
After I docked it.

On a planet so small
I hadn't expected
The days to be long.
It was hard to stay rested.

Up and then down,
The large sun did bounce.
Not fully setting,
Not even an ounce.

The day was so long,
Fifty- nine to be exact,
Before the sun set.
Finally I can nap!

I didn't have time
To stay another whole day,
So I picked up and went
And left behind the dull gray.

Eighty-eight days;
I left and checked orbit,
And noticed that I
Was back where I started.

# Venus

Venus is like
Earth's evil twin;
Similar in ways,
Yet different within.

They share the same size
And rocky terrain,
But that's kind of it.
They are not the same.

I worked out real hard
Preparing for this.
I stepped down outside
And fell to my fists.

Standing is hard here,
Gravity's so heavy!
And the heat is so bad,
I'm already sweaty!

I turned on the fan
I placed in my helmet,
Which only made me wish
I wasn't in this hell pit.

The clouds around me
Smell like rotten eggs.
I picked myself up,
And decided no thanks.

Imagining living here
For a full Venus day.
It'd feel like a year!
So I'm not gonna stay.

Volcanoes are bursting,
There are crushed up shells
Of robots last sent here
To document hell.

It's hot and it smells,
And I totally hate it!
To come here again,
I'd rather be sedated.

# Mars

We all know of Mars,
One way or another.
From movies and books,
Or a fan of the Rover.

My penpal lives here,
We've talked for a while.
We're meeting today
And I can't help but smile!

I don't really know
How to find Martians,
But Grommit had told me
Where they are hidden.

It's as cold as Antarctica
So I bundle up good,
And get ready to trek
The rusty desert on foot.

I get there by sundown,
My friend waits for me.
We happily greet each other
And sit down for some tea.

My Martian friend told me
Of plans to take Earth.
His people are desperate
To live on new turf.

"Go ahead," I replied,
His face now a smile.
"Most of us thought already
You were there for a while!"

Our visit lasted later
Than we originally planned.
We talked all night long,
It was really grand.

I shared my adventures
To the other planets,
And he shared as well,
"A Day In The Life of Grommit."

When the sun rose,
We bid our goodbyes.
We promised to share
Future things from our lives.

# Asteroid Belt

As I'm making my way
Through the solar system,
I've encountered some asteroids,
Barely missing them.

They rotate the sun
Just like the planets,
But are smaller in size
So we don't count it.

Millions of them
Surround me right now!
I'm concentrating hard
To avoid them somehow.

Faster and faster,
I'm getting the hang of this!
Till one hits me just right
Crash landing on Ceres.

# Ceres

This dwarf planet, Ceres,
Is smaller somehow
Than our own moon,
But it's where I am now.

I fix up my rocket
With duct tape and glue.
For luck I then add
Some W-42.

Then I remember
Something quite special;
This rock here I'm on,
Inspired the word "cereal!"

I go back inside,
And pour out in a bowl
Some cereal I saved
For this moment of gold.

I crunch a few minutes
Then also remember,
Those small clouds I see
Are just water vapor.

I take out my gadget
I made for this purpose,
And then I extract
The droplets for storage.

I walk for a bit,
Just wander around,
For I know my next stop
I won't see the ground.

Restocked and full belly,
I hop back on board.
The Gas Giant's next,
And I'm scared to the core.

16

# Jupiter

As I approach
This massive behemoth,
My stomach does flips
I start to get squeamish.

The sheer size of it
Is more than I fathom!
I fly towards inside
Where it feels like a chasm.

I know I can't land,
But need to go through it
And see what the clouds
Look like from within it.

I brace myself for
The force of the wind.
Swirling around,
Causing me to spin.

Then suddenly all goes still,
And I regain my thoughts.
I'm in the eye of the storm,
The Great Red Spot.

I take it all in,
I cannot believe
The live painting before me.
I never want to leave.

Incredible colors,
Dangerous sounds;
The haunting of Jupiter
Is all around.

I can't help but wonder
What's at the center
A planet that thrives?
Or a dark epicenter?

We may never know
What lies underneath
These raging storms
That hypnotize me

# Saturn

On lap twenty-four,
I race around the rings.
As I go, I think
About a lot of things.

Another gas giant,
Supposedly no life.
And it's so far away,
There isn't much light.

I'm wondering, though,
If I just dive to the middle
And see for myself
If the core is even little.

Out of nowhere it seems,
I take a hard left,
Slicing through the atmosphere,
To the very depth.

Getting darker and darker,
It doesn't seem possible,
My radar picks up
A small object that's probable.

I slow myself down,
And come to a halt.
I can't help but express
My shock to a fault.

Here in the center
Of the great planet Saturn,
Is a small small oasis,
That's life-like in pattern.

The core is only
The size of my hand,
But here it is clearly,
Proof of some land!

The closer I look,
I see a small ocean,
And visitors sailing
As if in slow motion.

I wonder if they see me
Through all the gas.
I hope they don't panic,
To see an alien at last.

# Uranus

In middle school science,
Uranus made us laugh.
Who would name a planet
Something so crass?

I thought of these jokes
As I made my way there.
Couldn't wait to tell my friends
How I would fare.

I bundle up good,
I heard it was cold.
Through moons left and right,
It was comedy gold.

Although it's of gas
Like Jupiter and Saturn,
There is known rock here,
But it couldn't be sadder.

Not a soul in sight,
I land on the ground.
There is snow everywhere,
So then I lay down.

The first snow angel ever
To be made in space!
I'm proud of myself,
Though it wasn't a race.

I explore a bit more,
And it's easy to see,
That nothing is here.
Uranus is empty.

# Neptune

Another ice giant,
But this one is darker.
I turn on my headlights
To light it up further.

What look like sea creatures
Look up to my light.
My heart just then stops,
And I feel fight or flight.

They are all "swimming"
Or riding the winds,
Just living their lives,
Until I sauntered in.

A creature came up
To my rocket's window,
And pressed its ugly face,
It fogged it up slow.

I'm not sure what to do,
As we watched each other's eyes.
I start to back up slowly,
And said a silent goodbye.

# Pluto

Unsettled and disturbed
By my last find,
I head over to Pluto,
A dwarf planet defined.

The first in the Kuiper Belt;
To be honest, my favorite.
Smaller than our moon,
And the most debates about it

Pluto was always a planet,
No matter what they say.
Bigger than Texas,
They can't take that away.

I ice skate across
That heart-shaped glacier,
Meeting Plutians who wave
From their icy skyscrapers.

It feels like vacation,
Though a little too cold
To come here and wander
The amazing globe.

I hiked up the mountains
Covered in red snow,
Then I looked to the blue skies
And knew it's time to go.

# Haumea

As homesick as I'm getting,
I've yet finished my quest!
For my journey through space
Still has a little way left.

Haumea the dwarf planet
Is shaped like an egg.
I wonder if it'll hatch
If it hears me beg.

So I make myself comfy,
And set up a camp.
I sit and I wait
And tell it, "you can."

Every day without fail,
I lay my hand down
And sense the vibrations
Of something underground.

Days and days pass,
It turns into months.
And finally one day,
I feel the cracks come.

I jump in my rocket,
Surprised and excited!
I lift off in time
Where the ground is now parted.

I fly far enough
To get a good view
Of the creature emerging
From its shell, on cue.

This cat-like being
Is ancient and old,
Yet just like a child
It's brazen and bold.

It reaches to stretch,
And lets out a yawn.
Then takes off to space
To find where it's from.

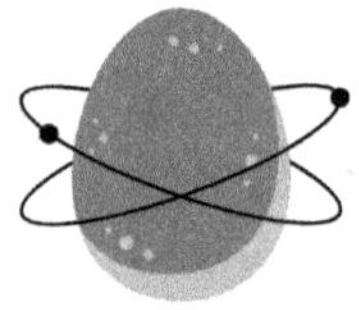

# MakeMake

Another dwarf planet,
Its name's MakeMake!
I heard that its nickname
Is the Easter bunny.

I thought that was strange,
Didn't think there's a reason.
Turns out that out here,
It's always Easter Season.

Although it's so cold,
Pastel colors are everywhere,
As space bunnies hop
With baskets to share.

I'm given one myself,
And asked to join the hunt!
Looking for decorated eggs,
And not just for fun.

This is their life force,
A way to survive.
If they stop they will freeze,
And most likely die.

# Eris

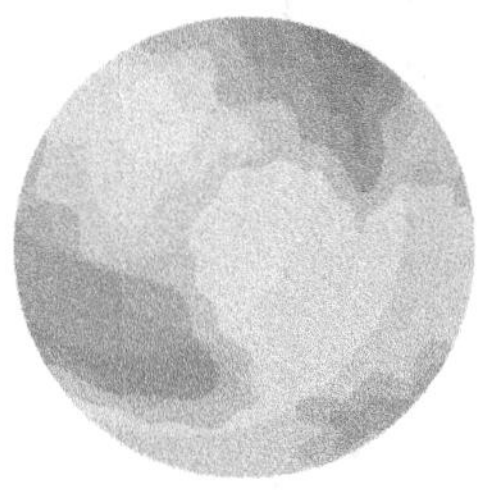

I'm a little bit bitter,
Visiting this place,
For it is the reason
That Pluto's displaced.

In recent years,
More objects were discovered
Inside the Kuiper Belt;
Another then another.

Too small for a planet,
Too big as just a rock.
Eris sparked interest
For dwarf planet talk.

The citizens here
Do not quite like that.
They are proud of their planet,
And don't care to chat.

They live out their lives
And know their own worth!
They don't need to impress
The people of Earth.

# The Ort Cloud

The end of our solar system,
It's so very far!
With even more dwarf planets
Than we've discovered so far.

Surrounded by comets
And asteroids alike,
To get through this cloud
Will be a big fight.

What's on the other side?
We have no clue!
For discovery's sake,
Go through it, I'll do.

Trillions of objects
To dodge and avoid,
Defeating this challenge
Is my own choice.

# Planet X

Emerging from the Ort,
I couldn't believe my eyes!
In the distance sat Earth,
Floating peacefully in the skies.

I approach with caution,
But curiosity wins.
I get a better look
At Earth's massive twin.

Completely untouched
By humanity's hand,
I enter the atmosphere
And settle on dry land.

It truly is quiet.
No animals or humans,
No bustling cities,
Or ancient sights of ruins.

I flew around it for months,
Just looking for a soul.
Then finally one day,
I met one, who told,

"This planet was built
As a backup for yours,
But the way Earth's been treated
Has closed that door.

Humans are terrible,
They just take and they take
Until there's nothing left,
And your atmosphere bakes.

You've done this to yourselves,
I have no pity for you.
You don't deserve another chance,
And you know that's the truth."

I beg and I plead
And I make my case,
Not totally prepared
To save the human race!

"I can't tell you you're wrong,
But you're also not right.
We humans have lived
And survived out of spite.

We live for our loved ones,
We'd do anything for.
The majority of us
Are just haggard and poor.
We try to be peaceful,
But those in charge,
Make life so much harder
For us while they're at large.

There will always be
Bad apples among us,
And the ones that we have
Are the ones who have screwed us.

So I think I can say
On behalf of us Earthlings
We can leave those ones there
To suffer their own doings"

The little green man
Thought for a moment
Then nodded his head
And gave his consent

# Return to Earth

I got back in my rocket
And zoomed really fast,
To share with the world
We're saved at last!

I went through the Ort Cloud,
And passed the constellations,
And picked up dear Grommit
To prove my revelations.

When I landed on Earth,
I was greeted by the president
I said, "Listen sir,
I have news most precedent."

I spent the afternoon
Sharing my findings,
And told of the agreement,
The president obliging.

The world soon found out
This miraculous plan,
And Grommit went out
To test who's a good man.

Turns out there's a loophole,
And many deep down
Are actually good people
But can't rid of their frown.

So most of us went,
Except for the psychopaths,
To New Earth to live
New lives with good impact.

# Coming Home

The journey was harrowing,
We lost some along the way,
To the other planets
Where some wanted to stay.

But many of us continued,
Determined to survive
To the brand new world
Where we can truly thrive.

I sent my friend Grommit
To retrieve fellow Martians,
To share this new planet
Together in good terms.

Seeing what Earth
Really should have been,
Is beautiful and tragic.
We grieved for it then.

We all came together
And agreed on the spot,
That we'd treat this one nicer
And be grateful for what we've got.

We learned from our mistakes
And took care of each other.
We treasured New Earth,
And lived happily ever after!

www.ingramcontent.com/pod-product-compliance
Lightning Source LLC
LaVergne TN
LVHW010824200726
843508LV00012B/2490